Activities We Do

We Take Care of Pets

by Nick Rebman

FOCUS READERS

SCOUT

www.focusreaders.com

Focus Readers is distributed by North Star Editions:
sales@northstareditions.com | 888-417-0195

Produced for Focus Readers by Red Line Editorial.

Photographs ©: PeopleImages/iStockphoto, cover, 1; LightField Studios/Shutterstock Images, 4; unguryanu/Shutterstock Images, 7; Impact Photography/Shutterstock Images, 9 (top); Markus Gann/Shutterstock Images, 9 (bottom); EniSine/Shutterstock Images, 11, 16 (bottom left); Poprotskiy Alexey/Shutterstock Images, 13, 16 (top left); Monika Wisniewska/Shutterstock Images, 15 (top); CC7/Shutterstock Images, 15 (bottom), 16 (bottom right); 9dream studio/Shutterstock Images, 16 (top right)

Library of Congress Cataloging-in-Publication Data
Names: Rebman, Nick, author.
Title: We take care of pets / by Nick Rebman. |
Description: Lake Elmo, MN : Focus Readers, [2020] | Series: Activities we do
Audience: K to grade 3. | Includes index.
Identifiers: LCCN 2018057173 (print) | LCCN 2018060026 (ebook) | ISBN 9781641859981 (PDF) | ISBN 9781641859417 (ebook) | ISBN 9781641858038 (hardcover) | ISBN 9781641858724 (pbk.)
Subjects: LCSH: Pets--Juvenile literature.
Classification: LCC SF416.2 (ebook) | LCC SF416.2 .R43 2020 (print) | DDC 636.088/7--dc23
LC record available at https://lccn.loc.gov/2018057173

Printed in the United States of America
Mankato, MN
May, 2019

About the Author

Nick Rebman enjoys reading, walking his dog, and traveling to places where he doesn't speak the language. He lives in Minnesota.

Table of Contents

Pets Are Fun

We love pets.

We take care of them.

Pets need to play.

We run with them.

We give them **toys**.

toy

Staying Clean

Pets need to stay clean.

We brush our cat.

We give our dog a bath.

This pet lives in a **cage**.

We keep the cage clean.

cage

Jobs Every Day

Pets need to eat every day.

We fill a **bowl** with water.

We fill a bowl with food.

bowl

We take the dog outside.

We pick up the waste.

We throw away the waste.

Then we **wash** our hands.

wash

Glossary

bowl

toys

cage

wash

Index